PEACE 101

from the Spiritual Living Series

Other Books by Calvin Witcher

PARENTING WITH PIECES

150 DAYS OF PEACE

THE 5 STEP RELATIONSHIP BLUEPRINT

PEACE 101

TELL THEM

Other Co-Authored Books with Calvin Witcher

The Better Business Book

CalvinWitcher.com

PEACE 101

from the SPIRITUAL LIVING SERIES

CALVIN WITCHER

WITCHER
PUBLISHING GROUP

PEACE 101: from the Spiritual Living Series

Published and distributed by Witcher Publishing Group.

Contributing Editor: Jeremy Witcher
Cover Design: Calvin Witcher
Interior Design: Calvin Witcher

This book may be purchased in bulk for educational, business, fundraising, or sales promotional use. For Information, please email info@witcherpublishing.com

Publishing consultation, support, design, and composition by Witcher Publishing Group. www.witcherpublishing.com.

Library of Congress Cataloging-in-Publication Data

Trade Paperback ISBN: 978-0-9971151-8-5
E-book ISBN: 978-0-9971151-9-2

Because of the dynamic nature of the Internet, any web addresses or links contained in this book may have changed since publication and may no longer be valid. The views expressed in this work are solely those of the author and do not necessarily reflect the views of the publisher, and the publisher hereby disclaims any responsibility for them.

Witcher Publishing Group - rev. date: 03/05/2017

Witcher Publishing Group
Visit WitcherPublishing.com

Table of Contents

Outlined Overview

I. **PEACE**
   a. **Acceptance**
      i. **Awareness**
         1. **Why** Do We Need To Be Aware?
         2. **How** Do We Become Aware?
            a. **Helps To Awareness**
            b. **Hindrances To Awareness**
      ii. **Neutrality**
         1. **Why** Do We Need Neutrality?
         2. **How** Do We Become Neutral?
            a. **Helps To Neutrality**
            b. **Hindrances To Neutrality**

   b. **Balance**
      i. **Why** Do We Need Balance?
      ii. **How** Do We Become Balanced?
         1. **Helps To Balance**
         2. **Hindrances To Balance**
      iii. **What** Are The **Elements** Of Balance?
         1. **Visual** – depth, velocity, and motion perception.
         2. **Vestibular System** (inner ear)

from the Spiritual Living Series

Introduction

❖

Hello Beloved. Thank you for joining me on this journey into understanding peace. You will find that many of the terms we use here in this material are familiar. The tendency might be to say, "I already know that." Try to resist that temptation. There is always something new that can come forth.

My challenge to you is to allow yourself to see and understand these concepts from a new perspective. Don't restrict your own growth simply because of familiarity.

Come with an open mind.

In time, you may come to understand these principles more fully.

About The Format

I have provided space in this format to write down your thoughts, goals and questions. I have also given opportunity for you to physically reinforce definitions by writing them down. There is a benefit to physically writing down an idea. Your whole body gets to participate in the experience and from that experience new patterns of thinking and behaving emerge.

from the Spiritual Living Series

Inspirational Quote

"Follow peace with all men, and holiness, without which no man shall see the Lord."

– Hebrews 12:14

How we understand and interpret peace in our own practical experience makes all the difference in how we integrate with those around us.

Let's face it. We can all use more peace. And we need to practice peace.

I believe that there are some steps that help lead us to peace. I have witnessed these steps work in my own life and in the lives of those I work with. No matter what the struggle or the crisis, there is a path where peace can prevail.

PEACE

is not the same as lack of war

from the Spiritual Living Series

Just because you are a person of peace doesn't mean that you will not face challenges or "war" times. You will hit points of difficulty. Peace does not mean that all things in your life are great.

We need to shift our thinking away from *peace = perfect*.

I want to help you do this. We can understand how to use peace and find peace in all circumstances when we understand that peace is something other than constant harmony.

Disagree?

Well, let's say that peace is the opposite of war. How many wars are in your life? So, you win one war and have peace in that area. What about the other areas? You could see how you can jump from war to war trying to find peace in everything only to be at continual war with everything.

In order to stop this destructive cycle, I want you to separate the idea of war vs. peace. I want you to go internally and find what peace looks like for you *despite* what wars are raging around you. Frankly, there will always be some war or resistance to go through or experience. However, you don't have to allow every war to destroy your peace. In fact, you can find peace in the middle of a war.

We are connected and interconnected to everything around us. This is good. But, not everything around us is immediately good for us. What is good for one being, at one time in their existence, may not be the best for you in this particular time and existence.

Oftentimes, we confuse peace with having to control others. We view them as our "war" and we try to stop, control, or change them to bring relief or peace into our own experience. I want to teach you how to find your own relief or peace in all circumstances.

Really, all of this goes down to an internal vs. external perspective. If you need for everything external to be correct before you can have peace, you are going to be a slave to your external environment.

"Knowledge makes a man unfit to be a slave."
– Frederick Douglas[i]

from the Spiritual Living Series

I want to give you the knowledge that frees you from the victimhood mentality of reacting to your external environment. Common sense is not common practice, as I always like to say. So, in times where we are unable to move ourselves in a progressive direction, we need to stop and understand what it is we are trying to achieve. In doing so, we can find steps or processes that unlock the answers we are looking for.

How would you put these ideas into your own words?

_____

_____

_____

_____

_____

_____

_____

_____

What are some examples you can think of where the "lack of war" has not caused peace?

_____

_____

_____

_____

_____

_____

Peace is _____ the same as

_____ of _____.

So, What Is Peace?

❖

My definition of peace is...
"a state of order by the use of **Acceptance** and **Balance**."

Order can be seen as a systematic way of doing things – a way of putting things into their place. Order is finding a way to categorize or prioritize situations or people, so that they can be understood by us. Our understanding then allows for safe and effect actions.

I want to point out that our understanding that categorizing and prioritizing situations or people is personal. Each of us will have a slightly different perspective on how and what to categorize. We also will have different priorities. This is ok. We want to find out what works for you.

That being said, if we do not order our existence, then we introduce chaos into our life. Anytime we have chaos in our life we don't allow acceptance to come forth. If we do not have acceptance, we have resistance and, if we have resistance, we are at war.

Order is the foundation of everything. Even chaos has its own order. *But, more about that later.*

When we talk about order we are talking about a structure that allows for patterns to be effective for us. This allows for us to create a pattern where we can understand and accept peace.

What does order look like for you?

_____

_____

Take a moment to put your life into categories. *Example; Personal Goals, Family, Friends, Work etc.* Each of these will, of course, have subcategories. Be as specific or general as you want.

_____

_____

_____

_____

_____

Now, briefly prioritize these categories. There is no right or wrong answer. Be careful to truthfully prioritize your categories according to what *you feel* should be first and not what others think should be first. Remember – you are trying to find your order.

_____

_____

_____

_____

Peace is a state of _____ by the use of _____ and _____.

Acceptance

Acceptance is not the same as agreement.

There is a common misunderstanding that acceptance is the same thing as agreement. Let me be clear. Acceptance is ***not*** the same thing as agreement.

A psychological definition of acceptance is "recognizing a process or condition without attempting to change it."[ii] The concept is close in meaning to 'acquiescence', derived from the Latin 'asquiescere' (to find rest in). The term acceptance (as we are using it) is not the same as agreement.

I think confusion comes because we view the act of accepting as giving some sort of permission. Usually when we give someone permission, it is because we agree with the activity or thought being presented. Yes, acceptance does have an overtone of permission, but what are we giving permission for? We are giving permission for **us** to be at rest. This is again an internal focus rather than an external focus. We are giving ourselves the permission to be without "war". And, while we previously stated that the lack of war does not automatically bring us peace, the lack of war does place us in circumstances that are more favorable to peace.

Indeed, it is especially important to find internal rest in the face of external unrest. We want to get to the point of being able to "see" an idea or situation and give ourselves the permission to say, "it is what it is". We do this without trying to change what we "see". We give ourselves the permission to rest apart from that situation or idea.

What areas can you "see" that you don't agree with?

_____

_____

_____

_____

How can you be at rest with what "is" without trying to change it?

_____

_____

_____

_____

Acceptance is _____ a process or condition _____ attempting to _____ it.

You must be aware of yourself and your surroundings for you to find rest in any situation or thought.

from the Spiritual Living Series

Awareness

Awareness is the ability to directly know and perceive, to feel, or to be conscious of events, objects, thoughts, emotions, or sensory patterns.

In this level of consciousness, sense data can be **confirmed** by you (the observer) without necessarily implying experiential understanding.

Awareness is to "see".

Why Do We Need To Be Aware?

We cannot change, understand, or balance what we do not know is exists. If you do not see something it does not exist for you. If it doesn't exist, then there is nothing to change.

Most of us want external change before we internally change. We are doing it backwards. Even external change comes from internal change.

Often, we have not considered what it is within us that we want to change. Now you might say, "I thought you didn't want us to change things." Not necessarily. By reading this material, you are asking to change something about you. You want more peace, which might be a change from your current reality. I am not asking you to never produce change. I am asking you to change those things that are changeable – which is you. We might effect change in others as we come into contact with them. But, the influence we have on others only amplifies what is inside us. Well then, you might say, "I am going to change myself so I can get others to finally change." It doesn't work like that. You need to let go of the idea of changing others and refocus your energies and your awareness to yourself – period. There is no other way to find peace. And honestly, this path is the best for you and for others.

So, I want to give you the tools to refocus your energies inward, in order to give you the internal change you want.

What are some internal things you are aware of? (Negative and Positive.)

_____

_____

_____

_____

_____

_____

_____

How can you accept the negative aspects of what you see in yourself? (Refer to our definition of acceptance.)

_____

_____

_____

_____

_____

How Do We Become Aware?

Helps To Awareness

Quieting Your Mind – A mind full of noise will produce chaotic results. This goes back to priority and order. You can only efficiently focus on one or two tasks at a time. You can only productively process a few ideas at a time.

Our brains are fast – incredibly fast – but even our brains categorize, prioritize and set limits on how much is entering our experience and how fast it comes to our attention. Most of our brain's job is to filter out what it perceives is unnecessary.

If we constantly allow external stimuli (which is infinite) to overwhelm our mind, we will never know who we are or what we are doing. We will inevitably conform who we are to whom those around us are. We will only react and never act.

Practices like meditation and other quieting techniques help facilitate focus or "seeing" and relieve the stress on our body's filtration system. By doing this, our body and mind can put energies towards growth instead of survival.

from the Spiritual Living Series

What are some methods you want to use to quiet your mind?

_____

_____

_____

_____

Slowing Down – By slowing down we give ourselves a chance to make an informed decision. I am not saying that everything must be slow. But especially if you find yourself struggling with a certain topic, then taking the time to practice and mastering that topic is beneficial. And the best way to do that is slow down. Think of any developmental process. You always start out slow and then gain momentum. And, even once you have achieved a level of mastery on a subject, many find that slowing down occasionally, allows for maintenance and retuning.

What are some methods you want use to slow down?

_____

_____

_____

_____

Sensory Development – Here we are asking ourselves the question, "What am I experiencing and how am I experiencing it?" We are looking to find clues through our senses to understand what we are processing. We then can make effective decisions on what we need to include or exclude in our physical experience in order to move us toward our intended goal. The only way to do this is by paying attention to each sense as we use it. Ask yourself the 'who, what, when, where and why' questions. Do this with each sense until you are a master at deciphering what your body is trying to tell you.

What sense do you want to work on? What are the questions you want to ask yourself as you pay attention to that particular sense?

_____

_____

_____

_____

Hindrances To Awareness

Hyper Fixation (mental) – This is a person who can't see the forest for the trees. They are always looking at each detail and getting lost in those details that they create an overwhelming experience for themselves. In turn, they often shut down and quit because they do not know how to systematically achieve their goals. They may have good intentions but they are unable to execute big ideas because of their perfectionistic tendencies. They are mentally too busy.

Hyper Vigilance (physical) – This is a person who must be physically busy all the time. Here we find a person never physically resting for more than a few seconds before they are off running to do some other activity. They feel there is no need to stop and reset. This can be demonstrated by physical jitters or body movement or activities placed back, to back, to back with no balancing rest. This person can use activity to distract themselves from themselves.

Limiting Habits – This is any pattern that blocks what we feel, hear, or understand. Because this person uses people and things to limit their experience they block their internal awareness. Different from the idea of filtering which choses a priority of focus, these people resist to ever focus on what they do not like or understand. "I can't" is often in their vocabulary.

Substance Abuse – This is anything that dulls or heightens focus and awareness to the point of unbalance and chaos. I will include everything and anything in this category – including one's thoughts. Yes, it does also include the traditional substances that any society abuses. But don't think that just because you don't drink, smoke, etc. that you are free and clear. Anything in a person's life that is used to incite a chaotic experience could be potentially abused. Dulling senses and heightening senses are not necessarily negative but one must carefully ask the question of why this is being done. If we are looking to escape ourselves, this is a clear indication that we are abusing this substance, thought, or idea.

Awareness is the ability to directly _____ and _____, to feel, or to be conscious of _____, objects, _____, _____, or _____, patterns.

What are two areas you would like to accept that you have been avoiding?

_____

_____

_____

_____

_____

_____

_____

_____

What awareness do you already have? Celebrate areas you can "see".

_____

_____

_____

_____

What "Helps" are you going to use to become aware?

_____

_____

_____

_____

What "Hindrances" are you going to avoid to become aware?

_____

_____

_____

The next component of acceptance is neutrality.

Neutrality is holding a position of undecided views. Physically speaking, neutrality is having a state of being chemically and electrically balanced.

Neutrality

Why Do We Need Neutrality?

If you are like many, you might have a knee jerk reaction when someone brings up the subject of neutrality. The very subject sounds boring or at best passive. What fun is that? Well, if you will give me just a moment I think you will soon see how learning the art of neutrality can liberate you from your limiting patterns. Neutrality is a powerful tool which is often overlooked.

Neutrality allows an expansion of our awareness. It also allows us to make safe and effective choices.

Without neutrality, we react to everything around us. Neutrality allows us to bring all the information about a topic into focus without jumping the gun or reacting because certain information has been given such focus. Again, you cannot make informed choices if you are unwilling to even be presented with the information to make a choice. You cannot change, develop, or direct what you cannot see.

The problem with neutrality is that we are born with our own perspective. Just by us being us we bring our own biases and views. Neutrality is not something that comes easily to humans. So then how do we become neutral?

What areas in your life are neutral?

_____

_____

_____

_____

What areas in your life are not neutral?

_____

_____

_____

_____

How Do We Become Neutral?

Helps To Neutrality

Making No Comment – Make no comment. This may sound simple enough but the practice is far from it. Try going a day without giving your opinion. Try even an hour. Not very easy, is it?

We have been programed to give our opinion on everything, from who should wear what, to the best meal to serve Friday night. We have a current cultural environment that values quantity of opinions over quality of those opinions. Often it is these opinions that bombard and clutter our experiences. As we have seen, a cluttered mind is counter-intuitive to peace. So, why do we feel the need to always give our opinion?

Opinions make us feel valued. Opinions also make us feel like we are engaging in a process. They make us feel like we are doing something or changing something. But, opinions rarely do what we think they do. Ask yourself this question. After you have commented on a topic then what typically happens? Well, someone usually comments back. They either agree with you, which causes you to affirm your belief, or they disagree with you which causes you to affirm your belief. What change has been made? None. Often an exchange of opinions deteriorates into a fight – either against a person directly or against a group of people indirectly.

When we practice making no comment, we end useless cycles. Who knows, we might even learn something.

Have you ever refrained from commenting? What happened?

Understanding Perspectives – Here we are asking ourselves what does it look like to be in someone else's shoes? How does this situation or action affect them? What are they experiencing? What can I learn from what they say?

Tell about the last time you stopped to think about the perspective of someone else?

Hindrances to Neutrality

Pride – One of the biggest hindrances to neutrality is pride. When we think that we are better than someone else, or our perspective is more important, we have locked ourselves into a holding pattern. These self-imposed patterns block information from entering our experience. Why? Because we think we already know everything there is to know.

Have you ever put aside your pride in a situation? What happened?

Physical or Mental Separation – Anything that presents itself as separation will work against neutrality. A separation mindset focuses on the difference between opposing elements. When we focus on the differences we are asking ourselves to accept more if we want peace. And if we are struggling with accepting the situation to begin with, focusing on the separation that the situation represents can be overwhelming.

But, sometimes there is a separation and we don't know why. Sometimes a simple geographic presence such as a train track or a mountain is enough to give us the illusion of "us" vs. "them". Being aware of our surroundings and the feelings that go with those surroundings can help us see what is going on. Separation can also be mental. Language barriers can cause a mental separation. In each case, moving past the elements that separate can be a step to viewing the information from a neutral perspective.

Have you ever experienced physical or mental separation?

_____

_____

_____

_____

What did you learn from these experiences?

_____

_____

_____

_____

Past Trauma Patterns – A trauma is something that has not been resolved in our lives. This is something that we deem negative. It has stopped our growth. This is a natural way of us protecting ourselves. But often because we are trying to protect ourselves we are judgmental, dogmatic and offensive to other people. So, sometimes we must go back and heal our past trauma to allow neutrality.

What past traumas are you healing from?

_____

_____

_____

_____

Have there been traumas that have been resolved? If so, how did this free you?

_____

_____

_____

_____

What two areas would you be willing to neutralize?

_____

_____

_____

_____

What neutral subjects or experiences do you want to avoid because you are not neutral?

_____

_____

_____

_____

What two hindrances to neutrality are you going to practice resolving?

_____

_____

_____

_____

Neutrality allows an _____ of our

_____ and allows us to make

_____ and _____ choices.

The secondary component of peace is **Balance**.

Balance

What Is Balance?

Balance is a distribution of elements or energies resulting in synergetic proportions.

From the time we were young, we were working on our balance: to roll over, pull ourselves up, crawl, walk, and ride a bike. But, have you ever stopped and thought why we need to balance? Balance is more than just the accomplishment of staying upright. Balance is in fact the cycle of life. For every up, there is a down; every in, an out; every dark, a light. Balance allows for safe, continuous and effective energy flow.

How Do We Become Balanced?

Helps To Balance

Understanding – To balance anything, we must understand what it is we are balancing. The speed, momentum, force, and pull will change from item to item; subject to subject. Understanding the full picture of what elements or subjects we are balancing is key to being able to balance. Take for example juggling. A feather, baseball, hula-hoop, and bowling ball all have different properties to consider when approaching how to juggle them. Also, one would want to know how many of each item were being juggled and if there were a certain combination mix. Were we juggling all balls or is there a hoop thrown in for good measure?

Pick a situation or topic that you have been working on during this process. How could understanding more about the situation or topic improve your balance regarding that situation or topic?

Practice – Next, we would need to practice, practice, practice. Consistent skill takes dedication, time and practice. Likewise, if you have not been used to practicing any of the elements of peace, *including balance*, you are going to need to give yourself specific and manageable areas of which you can practice.

How are you going to implement opportunities to practice balance?

_____

_____

_____

_____

_____

Hindrances To Balance

Preference Domination – This is when a person's preference is forced in a dominating way onto everyone around them with no consideration to how it might affect others. For instance, if I like chocolate ice-cream, I might think that everyone should like chocolate ice-cream. For me chocolate is the best taste there is. Why would anyone want to try anything else? Now, this is a silly example, but I think you get the point. Now what if I give chocolate ice-cream to someone who was allergic to chocolate ice-cream. What may have started out as me sharing my wonderful experience has turned into a horrible experience for someone else. All because I thought my choice should dominate everyone else's choices.

Have you ever used preference domination? Have you had preference domination used against you?

What Are The Elements Of Balance?

We can learn more about balancing by looking at how our human systems balance. We said that we start working on our balance from the time of birth, but what is happening?

First let's talk about our sight or visual balance.

The visual system deals with depth, velocity, and motion perception. Visual input from the eyes send the brain information about the position of the body relative to other objects, their depth, velocity and motion.

The spiritual application is that what we see impacts us greatly. What we "see" with our inner mind will either cause stability or unbalance. Yes, sometimes we will see things that throw us off. That is normal. But, if we are constantly finding ourselves proverbially tripping and falling because we are spiritually losing our balance, then we need to ask ourselves some questions.

First, am I able to see correctly. Just like our physical eyes, sometimes our vision needs to be corrected.

Secondly, if I can see correctly, then am I using the vision that I do have to keep me stable or am I distracted from what is right in front of me. Having good eyesight does you no good if you have your eyes closed.

Thirdly, if you have good vision and are paying attention yet still you are having balancing issues, then maybe your focus is off. Just like watching a scary movie and having bad dreams, you can put focus on things that are designed to unsettle you. In this case, you need to turn your focus to things that build you up not break you down.

How is your spiritual vision?

_____

_____

_____

_____

What improvements would you like to make to your spiritual vision?

_____

_____

_____

_____

The next human balancing system is the Vestibular System (inner ear). The most important part of human balance is the inner ear (which contains three canals). In simple terms, the three canals contain a gel-like liquid called endolymph and tiny hair cells. When both inner ears are working properly they give the brain information through the central nervous system about linear and angular positions of the body with respect to gravity. The eye and the ears complement each other not only to maintain balance, but also to maintain clear vision during movement. The inner ear sends impulses that continuously adjust your eyes in coordination to even the smallest movement of the body such as your heartbeat or breathing. This is a very cool process.

The spiritual application again is that what we hear plays directly into how we balance. Our spiritual inner ear works in conjugation with our sight to tell us what action to take. If we are not listening, we will never get the information that we need to make safe and effective choices. Now you can start to see that finding space to be still and listen is crucial to our spiritual growth and well-being.

How is your spiritual hearing?

_____

_____

_____

_____

What improvements would you like to make to your spiritual hearing?

_____

_____

_____

_____

The next system is the somatic sensory or somatosensory system (proprioception and exteroception). The Somatosensory System provides the brain two valuable pieces of internal and external spatial information to maintain balance. One comes from internal sensors within the body called propriceptors. Proprioceptors give the central nervous system information about the movement of body parts in relation to other parts of the body. This is called the sense of proprioception. Without the sense of proprioception, you would not be able to put food in your mouth without visually watching your hand moving to your mouth. A common test for loss of proprioception is walking the line during a sobriety test by police officers. The other Somatosensory information the brain uses comes from external body sensors called exteroceptors. Exteroceptors are pressure sensors located in your feet and hands that provide external spatial information about the topography of the ground or support surface. Exteroception also helps in your overall balance system by relaying information about ground movement. An example would be the difference between standing on solid ground and sinking into mud. The body is truly an amazing thing!

The spiritual application is that each element of your spiritual body is important. Everything about you is connected. Saying that one part of you doesn't matter is foolish at best. Often, I have found that we can push the spiritually broken parts to the side. This is dangerous. We must take time to stop and repair whatever we know is out of line or needs healing. Our system was meant to work together as one unit. Pay attention to what your spiritual and physical body is telling you. Take a holistic approach, and in doing so you will find your balance better than ever.

Balance is a distribution of _____ or _____ resulting in _____ proportions.

We have talked about how we balance, but now let's talk about what are we usually balancing?

What Are We Usually Balancing?

Good and Bad

There are many things that we balance, but one of the most common balancing acts in today's society is the idea of good and bad. I see individuals often struggle with breaking damaging patterns simply because they have associated change with something that is evil or bad. They tell me they are fighting or resisting that which is bad. Many times, they don't know why the idea they are fighting is evil. They just resist because they are "supposed to". I have found in these situations to put some specific concrete definitions to what we call good and bad.

I define good as *anything that initiates or sustains growth.*

I define bad as *anything that initiates or sustains decay.*

Now that I have told you my definition of good and bad, let's look at how we come to understand good and bad in our human experience. So, how did we develop our understanding of what good and bad is?

from the Spiritual Living Series

Development of Good and Bad

The first way we find out what is growth or decay for us is by personal or internal experience. By that I mean something we know or find out for ourselves. As a baby, we take this job very seriously. Everything is to be touched, tasted and experienced. Some experiences (the baby finds out) give more joy and some the baby would rather not experience again. The baby tests the limits without judgement and tries different experiences and ways to handle those experiences. Eventually, the baby connects growth or "good" to an activity. The baby likewise connects decay or "bad" to uncomfortable experiences. This is the beginning of understanding good vs. bad.

What is a good thing that you found out for yourself?

_____

_____

_____

_____

_____

_____

What is a bad thing that you found out for yourself?

_____

_____

_____

_____

The next way we find out what is good or bad is from other's or external experience. Someone tells us what they found out (or experienced for themselves). Or, we see how someone reacts to a situation and draw conclusions based on what we perceive they are going through. Eventually we connect those experiences of others or our externally viewed experiences as either good or bad.

What is a good thing that you found out from others?

_____

_____

_____

_____

What is a bad thing that you found out from others?

_____

_____

_____

_____

The third way we form our understanding of good and bad is from our present perspective. As time goes on, we reevaluate the "truth" of what is good and bad. Many times, what we understand about good and bad changes. Sometimes this creates resentment and a sense of betrayal as we disagree with the good and/or bad of the past. However, if we understand that the good and bad of the past can shift to a different good or bad for today, we are more forgiving or understanding of past experiences and can move into the new experiences we want to have. This can be challenging to many because our experiences create beliefs.

What is a good thing that you are experiencing now?

_____

_____

_____

_____

What is a bad thing that you experiencing now?

_____

_____

_____

_____

How do your past **internal** good and bad experiences and your past **external** good and bad experiences play into what you are experiencing right now?

Experiences of Good and Bad Create Belief

All our experiences, good or bad, create what we believe. This is based on how you perceive, understand

and enact what you have experienced. Often, we don't live in a place of balance because we are trying to place our personal experiences onto others. This is impossible to do. At best, you can be a partial influence in creating other's beliefs as they watch you. But, ultimately the conclusions they make about you and your experiences are up to them. So, in the end it is futile to run around forcing your understanding on others. Being the full integration of your current understanding of good and bad is all you can do and is, in fact, the best thing each of us can do. Each of us must take our own, others, and currant experiences into consideration to constantly reshape and reform our personal good and bad (growth and decay) model from which to work from. Anything else will be unbalanced. And if we are unbalanced we will not be able to find peace.

Why Should We Balance Good and Bad?

Well, I just said that we will not be able to find peace in an unbalanced state. But, I want to also give you encouragement that good and bad are opposites of the same cycle and nothing to be afraid of. Good (growth) is the fuel of decay and bad (decay) is fueled by growth. You will not have one without the other. Many times, we are seeking one part of this whole at the exclusion of all else. Again, this is unbalanced and will create huge amounts of fear in your life. Resting in the assurance that there will always be something good and there will always be something bad can give you comfort in moving through your daily experiences.

Helps to Balance Good and Bad

Allowing our perspective to expand without regret will give us a balance. Also, this is one of the keys for finding peace. Staying in the moment and really seeing, hearing, feeling and sensing where we are will allow us to bring forth our best in this moment. As we start to project too far forward or too far backward, we can remind ourselves of what is and bring our awareness to living life in the now.

Hindrances to Balance Good and Bad

Rigidly holding to past perspectives will inevitably throw off our balance. Because, we are changing and life is changing, trying to force or hold back the ebb and flow of such energies will cause the destruction of ourselves. Working with and through these energies as they change will keep us healthy and full of peace.

Good is anything that _____ or

_____ _____.

Bad is anything that _____ or

_____ _____.

What are the good things in your life?

_____

_____

_____

_____

What are the bad things in your life?

_____

_____

_____

_____

_____

_____

_____

_____

What is a balance that you can find between your good things and bad things?

_____

_____

_____

_____

_____

_____

_____

_____

_____

_____

_____

_____

_____

_____

Conclusion

Thank you for joining me on this journey into peace. I want to congratulate you for dissecting the elements of peace with me. Great job!

Celebrate the areas in your life where you are thriving in peace and continue working on those areas where you might be need an infusion of peace.

Keep in touch and give me the feedback on how this information has helped you in your personal experience. I look forward to hearing from you.

I want to conclude by reminding you that peace is not a just a point that you get to but a process of life. You will always be working on your peace and finding and re-finding the center of your peace. Keep doing the work and together we will create a better world.

Conclusion

Meet The Author

CALVIN WITCHER is an Author, Teacher and Spiritual Crusader that has coached international teachers, doctors, therapists, business professionals and individuals seeking clarity. Known for his bold and integrative approach to spirituality, he calls all to freedom and the soul's highest calling.

As a gifted counselor and speaker, the core of Calvin's message is "helping others find clarity through challenge, crisis, and change". Transcending socioeconomic and denominational barriers, his message resonates among people from every walk of life.

With a faith undaunted by the task at hand, this husband, father, and mentor is the prophetic voice to a progressive generation. Today, as a much-in-demand speaker and proclaimer of inclusivity and interfaith, he continues to fulfill his mission to radically heal and transform lives.

Calvin Witcher is available for speaking, teaching, consulting and counseling. For media inquiries, ideas for collaboration and more information, **please visit CalvinWitcher.com**

from the Spiritual Living Series

More Products and Offerings from Calvin

❖

Books

PARENTING WITH PIECES

150 DAYS OF PEACE

THE 5 STEP RELATIONSHIP BLUEPRINT

from the Spiritual Living Series

150 Days of Peace
– Devotional & Journal –

Over 4 Months of Daily Exercises and Encouragement that Creates a Life of Abundant Peace, Clarity, and Harmony

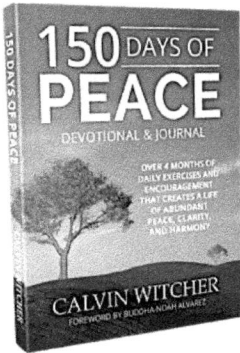

How do we form new habits? The simple answer is practice. Many of us desire to get rid of negative habits and create new positive habits. Whatever we desire to see in our life, we must put the structure in place to support our needs and wants.

150 Days of Peace – Devotional & Journal is a step-by-step process for creating more peace, clarity, and harmony throughout your day.

This daily devotional and journal is designed to guide you into a thriving and transformed life.

With loads of quotes and commentary, this book is the starting point for a successful day. We all desire a roadmap that leads us from our present problems to a place of power and peace. This book maps out the way.

ENJOY THE JOURNEY AS IT CONTINUALLY UNFOLDS.

Get Your Copy At CalvinWitcher.com or Wherever Books Are Sold

from the Spiritual Living Series

Parenting with Pieces

Parenting As A Catalyst
For Personal Growth

Discover what progress REALLY looks like when you get YOUR needs met first!

Introducing Parenting with Pieces — a groundbreaking book that will accelerate your personal growth and radically improve your effectiveness as a parent — piece by piece.

Here's a sample of what you will learn from this book:

- How to eliminate thoughts that question your ability to be a "good parent"
- How to balance your personal needs with the demands of building a family
- How to use proven psychological tools to help resolve your internal conflicts
- How to break negative cycles that come from your childhood experiences
- How to achieve personal happiness by identifying patterns that exaggerate unnecessary stress in your life
- How to overcome self-criticism by redefining who you are as a parent
  and much more...

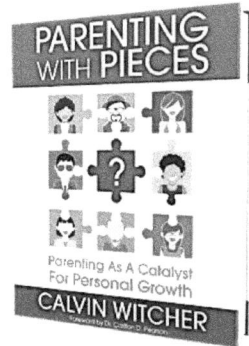

Get Your Copy At CalvinWitcher.com or
Wherever Books Are Sold

from the Spiritual Living Series

The 5 Step Relationship Blueprint

How To Create Conscious
And Connected Relationships

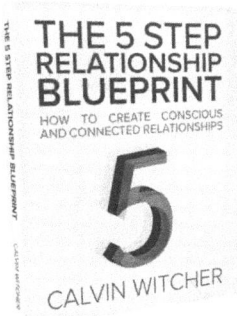

I know that relationships have their celebrations and they also have their challenges. The first thing I'd like for you to really seek to believe is that

you're not alone.

Experiencing challenges in your relationship does not make you weak – it makes you a worker. Anyone that is continually working on themselves and their relationship will inevitably encounter some rough patches.

This is normal.

May this offering serve as an investment in your relationship.

Get Your Copy At CalvinWitcher.com or
Wherever Books Are Sold

from the Spiritual Living Series

Work With Calvin

Coaching & Mentoring

Are you ready to embrace all that you were meant to be?

Calvin Witcher offers 1-on-1 sessions through holistic life coaching and spiritual mentoring. He will help you find clarity through every challenge, crisis and change of your life.

Are you searching for personal growth, professional development, or leadership training? Do you understand that there is more to your life than what you have been experiencing? Yes, you do! And, this is what you have been looking for! Your life will change for the better, and so too will the lives of those you impact.

Calvin Invites You To Experience Your Own Private Coaching Sessions.

★★★★★ Look at some of our 5-Star Yelp reviews![iii]

Alexander N.
Claremont, CA
3 friends
9 reviews

⭐⭐⭐⭐⭐ 7/8/2016

First to Review

Calvin exudes more positive energy than anyone I have ever met. His positive energy, his wisdom and his caring for creating positive change in others make him an extraordinary person. I am fortunate for the opportunity to know Calvin and to listen and apply his wisdom to my life.

Thank you Calvin for injecting your energy into our community. Keep up the great work!

Jack P.
Oakland, CA
0 friends
2 reviews

⭐⭐⭐⭐⭐ 10/10/2016

Calvin is an INCREDIBLE counselor and coach. He helped me go from overwhelm to deep, centered confidence and inner power. I'm so grateful for the work that we did together!

Are One-On-One Sessions For You?

- One-On-One Sessions Are For Individuals Incorporating Calvin's Principles Effectively, And Those Who Want To Keep Developing Their Experience To Fully Achieve Their Unique Destiny.

- One-On-One Sessions Are For Those Who Are Curious About An In-Depth Revelation Of Their Spiritual Awareness Their True God Nature.

- One-On-One Sessions Are For People Who Want To Create A Life That Reflects Their Core Beliefs But Are Aware Of A Gap Between How They Want

Things To Be And How They Currently Experiencing Their Reality.

- One-On-One Sessions Are For People That Have The Courage To Grow Despite Adversity, Change Even When It's Uncomfortable, And For People That Are Seeking To Live In Their Genius.

Audrey C.
Los Angeles, CA
1 friend
6 reviews

⭐⭐⭐⭐⭐ 8/1/2016

Calvin is extremely approachable, has a very positive attitude and a very unique approach to counseling and providing comfort to his clients. I consulted him on a few aspects on my relationship experiences and the suggestions he provided were very original and something I've never thought of to practice to achieve manifestation. His spiritual guidance and intuition guided me through a difficult time and I will definitely revisit again! Thank you Calvin:)!

Noah A.
Los Angeles, CA
4 friends
11 reviews

⭐⭐⭐⭐⭐ 7/9/2016

Clear-thinking, clear-seeing, and direct in action. These are the valuable, bold skills that Calvin utilizes in his guidance and every day connection. Not only does Calvin offer pointed energetic wisdom and spirit-centered solutions, but his words land high and have a unique way of nestling into the practical-positive, which lends toward genuine elevation in life, consciousness, and one's daily walk. I highly recommend Mr. Witcher for life coaching, intuitive business counsel, and spiritual development!

To submit your information to Calvin for coaching and mentoring, please visit CalvinWitcher.com

References

Unless otherwise indicated, all Scripture quotations are taken from the Bible.

[i] Goodreads - Goodreads Inc. -
http://www.goodreads.com/author/quotes/18943.Frederick_Douglass
[ii] Acceptance. (2016, November 30). In Wikipedia, The Free Encyclopedia.
Retrieved 16:53, March 6, 2017, from
https://en.wikipedia.org/w/index.php?title=Acceptance&oldid=752367250
[iii] Calvin Witcher Reviews. Yelp.com –
https://www.yelp.com/biz/calvin-witcher-dallas

Notes

❖

Notes

❖